A Century of Childhoods

Other works by Tony Connor

POETRY

With Love Somehow
Lodgers
12 Secret Poems
Kon in Springtime
In the Happy Valley
The Memoirs of Uncle Harry
Seven Last Poems from the Memoirs of Uncle Harry
New and Selected Poems
Spirits of the Place
Metamorphic Adventures
Things Unsaid: Selected Poems 1960-2005
The Empty Air

PLAYS

Billy's Wonderful Kettle
I Am Real and So Are You
The Last of the Feinsteins
A Couple with a Cat
Otto's Interview
Dr. Crankenheim's Mixed-Up Monster
Peace & Co.

A Century of Childhoods

Tony Connor

kin press

A CENTURY OF CHILDHOODS. Copyright ©2022 by Tony Connor. All rights reserved. No portion of this book may be reproduced, stored in a retrieval system, or transmitted in any form or by any means without prior written permission of the publisher, except for brief quotations used in critical reviews or articles, and certain other non-commercial uses.

Kin Press
kin-press.org
Higganum, CT 06441

Cover & interior design by J.C. Mlozanowski

ISBN: 978-0-9989293-5-4

Poetry / British
Early 20th Century / Childhood / Manchester, England

For my children—
Rebecca, Simon, and Samuel

A Century of Childhoods

Tony Connor

The poems in this volume are all based upon scenes from my childhood, or childhoods—remembered, imagined, and invented. The title of the sequence is an admiring nod to Thomas Traherne's *Centuries of Meditations*, written three hundred years ago.

—Tony Connor

Thoughts while dawdling down our street
to shop on Cheetham Hill Road:
"Might I be somebody else?"
Wondering who is thinking.

The fence against which I pushed
Alf Bennet to pummel him
with my little fists, knocking
the pink dummy from his mouth.

My mother chastising me
from an open top window
as I organised street games.
"Stop bullying those children!"

Mandley Park on a cold day.
The bowling green deserted,
two women with shopping bags,
a dog on its way somewhere.

Mr. Sharpe's reputation
as a good-humoured neighbour.
Long before his pot belly,
long before his shuttered house.

An after-smell of madness
pervading the wintry air
of the yard where an old man
was stabbed to death by his son.

An argument through the wall:
the rowdy couple next door
disputing nightly the cause
and nature of their dispute.

Cricket in an alleyway,
our side trailing by three runs.
Then a surprise boundary—
my sister's contribution.

Downright lies and concealment
recognized as defences
against suspicious parents
and other prying people.

Mrs. Goldberg in high heels,
puffing at a cigarette.
She and her handsome husband
stepping out for late cocktails.

Mistaken for the Micvah—
"4" instead of "44."
My sister at the front door
sending them to the milkbar.

An annex joining two rooms—
one step and the cellar door.
Cold air from another world,
spirits lingering unseen.

A solemn face in pencil,
drawn from a mirror image,
eyes of a stranger glancing
from mine to the page and back.

Large old houses among trees
at the end of long driveways,
footsteps light on wet gravel,
the end of my paper route.

Time wasted under gas-lamps,
fidgety feet, evening rain.
Grownups hurrying to catch
buses bound for the city.

Light and shadow trembling
among swags of summer leaves.
A quick stroll down Thomas Street,
toothache nagging at comfort.

Coal tumbling down the coalhole
into loud cellar darkness.
Dust hanging in the next room
where an old mangle rusted.

Hiding in the undergrowth
of an abandoned garden,
ignored by broken windows,
the empty mansion silent.

Mr. Feinstein's thick glasses.
Mrs. Pilling's stick-like legs.
Shirley's new breasts and swagger.
A biplane crossing the sky.

A boy with a mastoid hole,
a man who swung on crutches,
a kettle come to the boil,
a game played with spent matches.

Ballet dancers in Swan Lake.
Leaping and twirling midgets
on a tiny jewelled stage
far from my seat in the Gods.

Girls sly-whispering, laughing,
leaning closely together.
Boys kicking a ball about,
pretending not to notice.

Growing into a strange world,
yet a familiar place.
Fatherless and curious,
glad to be nobody else.

The two Hoffman daughters:
Brenda's unremarked beauty,
Daphne's slack-jawed gormlessness
eager to laugh at nothing.

All meanings muffled, secrets,
silences, nothing discussed,
nothing explained, no books read.
Day after day after day.

Night-shrieks. A woman running
down George Street. A man behind,
yelling at her in Yiddish.
My mother's sour frustration.

Standing between two milk churns
on Mr. Donnelly's cart.
Wheels clattering on cobbles.
Bessie's rump gleaming sweatily.

Hints of approaching illness:
lost property in a dream,
vivid hallucinations—
tarnished spoons, a train, ferrets.

Peered at through rusty railings:
pale children pushed in wheelchairs
along paths beneath trees
shading The Bethesda Home.

The stout corpse of Mrs. Bates
laid out in the front parlour,
air heavy with lily-stink,
a cloth covering her face.

Aimless walks, unfocussed thoughts,
up and down streets, through alleys,
onto crofts hung with washing,
round corners leading nowhere.

Rain bouncing off the fanlight.
An old, wind-up gramophone
repeating "Bye, bye blackbird"
through an empty afternoon.

Waking in the early hours,
bedroom moonlight-watery,
trains shunting in the distance,
body and mind ill at ease.

Things I didn't understand:
my father's disappearance,
mirror-depths where ghosts flitted,
the front door in full sunlight.

Winter. The outside privy
freezing cold in candlelight,
wind blowing through the loose door
on shaking, impatient flesh.

Things I thought I understood:
how to bowl flighted leg-breaks,
the purpose of metaphor,
the short cut to Crumpsall Lane.

Miss Bollington reciting
to the class in a cracked voice,
"Cuckoo, cuckoo, a merry note."
Our silent, sneering laughter.

Keeping deep thoughts to myself,
not knowing much about them,
or why they entered my head
insisting upon silence.

Tramcars no longer clanging
except in winter daydreams.
Their rails rusting in the roadway,
then being tarmacked over.

Inklings of understanding
outside Tobias's shop.
A sunny day, fun with friends,
old Ma Wragg shooing us off.

An attempt to say nothing
and make it seem like something:
a person on roller skates,
anonymous and unseen.

The dead, awaiting recall,
but appearing anyway:
Uncle Jack telling a joke,
Auntie May, false teeth clicking.

Albert Gladwin's burliness,
belied by his squeaky voice—
both used to put the wind up
children who didn't know him.

A downpour in the morning,
followed by sunshine and heat.
Steam rising from the old horse
in front of the coalman's cart.

Flagstone edges stepped over,
socks rolled identically,
a lamp post touched every day,
syllable-counts repeated.

Elderberries from our tree,
baked into a latticed pie
to be thrown in the dustbin
by my mother's second thoughts.

Official communiqués
from unimagined places.
Bombers overhead at night,
brick shelters in back streets.

Windy mornings in Woolworth's,
the library in winter,
a thin coat on a cold street,
squelchy black leaves underfoot.

A go-cart part-assembled
by argumentative boys,
who squabble about the wheels
and end up swopping punches.

Night on the upstairs landing,
and all the household asleep.
New moon framed in a skylight
as it moves across the town.

An imaginative leap
thought about for a long time
by someone incapable
of breaking settled habits.

The Great War twenty years gone:
maimed bodies, distant and small,
on the sunny balcony
of a convalescent home.

Episodes of happiness
unrecognized at the time,
reconstituted in bed
like fractured gleams edging sleep.

A fight in the school playground
between boys I didn't know.
Watching it from a corner,
mind busy with other things.

My sister and my mother—
unknown, alien creatures,
savaging each other's souls
as I stood there bewildered.

What could not be completed
after being well-begun;
something referred to proudly,
but with hints of self-contempt.

The Saturday matinee
at the Shakespeare Cinema:
hundreds of restless children
submitting to Flash Gordon.

Thoughts that wouldn't go away,
but wouldn't say what they meant.
Headaches and pains in the balls—
things I might have imagined.

Suggestive hints by grownups
talking of absent others;
Mr. Manton's gulped laughter,
Aunt Dorothy's warning glare.

A dead dog reappearing,
translucent in the bedroom
where it spent its living nights
curled up at my mother's feet.

The friend who lived in Bank Place—
his name, Timothy *something*—
a clever boy with buckteeth
and a badly knotted tie.

June afternoon in Coke Street,
ripples of heat from cobbles,
pungent bacon-and-cheese smells
filling Gilmore's little shop.

Racing myself at top speed
all the way down Park Terrace,
body one with its own rush,
eyes and mind the finish line.

Many troubled dreams drifting
from unhappy marriage beds
into the sooty darkness
between back-to-back houses.

Walking round and round near streets,
frightened to enter that house
where two monstrous females
fought in mockery of home.

People who kept to themselves
in the end house of our row:
a glum mother and father,
two boys with impetigo.

Clowes Park in February,
spongy ice at the lake's edge,
smoke rising from a bonfire
in the nursery garden.

The district's secret places,
resistant to broad daylight
and common understanding
of their ordinariness.

Spiritualist churches—
corrugated-metal shacks
in back streets—the services
attended by maiden ladies.

Early attempts at poems,
composed on rainy evenings
when I had nothing to do
but chase daft thoughts round and round.

Dirt beaten from a carpet
hung on a backyard clothesline,
my sideways leap to avoid
the speckled cloud dispersing.

Questions of identity
(a phrase learned light-years later):
my smiling face in the street,
my grim face in the mirror.

Wondering how Bessie Dunn
toppled me from Top of the Class—
a stumpy girl with straight hair
who acted like a nitwit.

Puddles in a long alley
reflecting midsummer sky
too large for such confinement,
too blue for dirty water.

End of the 60 bus route,
stone houses with moors above.
Whirr of insects in tall grass,
a picnic beside a weir.

Washing strung across The Back
on a good day for drying,
tethered billow of bedsheets,
slap and snap of wet linen.

Wolf Adler at the front door
of his family's dark house,
showing me a little box—
a "Mezuzah" he called it.

Things I knew nothing about—
meaning nearly everything;
negligible ignorance
set against rollicking games.

Taking in the Reverent Coop's
smarmy smile on the church steps
where he lingered to converse
with wealthy parishioners.

Summer days in the dapple
and cool shadow of plane trees,
hunting for caterpillars,
matchboxes at the ready.

An early love of reading—
The Wizard and the *Hotspur*—
first: "The Truth About Wilson,"
second: "The Wolf of Kabul."

Arthur knocking balls about
on the billiard table
stored in his parents' attic,
his feeble grasp of snooker.

Streets, alleys, crofts and ginnels
shifting position nightly
to trick unwary walkers
in my night after night dream.

A blackbird's trill at twilight
when I lay ill one summer—
like a song recollected
many years hence in old age.

Mr. Mounsor's "fish trousers,"
his mysterious rendezvous
with trawler-men in Grimsby,
from which he returned stinking.

Somebody going to bed
earlier than usual,
steep stairs ill-lit and chilly,
laughter from the living room.

A four-foot length of lead pipe
filled with a fibrous tree root—
source of a water-stoppage
unclogged by Alfred Hubbard.

An attempt to ascertain
what is irreducible
by wilfully forgetting
everything best remembered.

The lunatic asylum,
lonely in its leafy grounds;
snapshots of Uncle Harry,
stuck in there for twenty years.

Presences haunting our house,
anonymous, mute, unseen,
beside me in the kitchen,
on guard at my bedroom door.

Rusty stumps where railings stood
along the front garden wall—
ten, dangerous, upright spikes,
if I remembered rightly.

Premonitions of order,
looking like shoes in a row,
a birthday not forgotten,
hasty responses swallowed.

Kitchen gossip of women,
overheard with half an ear,
while I drew Nazi warplanes,
unnoticed at the table.

A cousin's secret affaire,
discovered and thwarted,
elopement with a lodger
stopped in its tracks at the door.

Gypsies spurned on the front step,
dirty palms refused silver;
curses accumulating
in housewives' horrified dreams.

A serenade at midnight
by a locked-out, drunken fool,
trying to regain the love
of a woman fast asleep.

Some people who moved slowly:
grandma leaning on my arm,
club-footed Alf Williams,
two bent old men with ruptures.

A lonely lake at nightfall,
glitter-wake of a moorhen
on sombre, silent water.
Houselights shining through the trees.

A fall and recovery,
spokes spinning beside my head,
grazed palms, torn trousers—the bike
jerked back upright, front wheel bent.

Everything clearly named
yet everything secret,
hidden within its name.
A world without understanding.

About the author

Tony Connor was born in 1930 and raised in a largely Jewish, working-class area of Manchester, England. When he was five, his father abandoned the family and Connor never saw him again. He left school at the age of fourteen and was apprenticed to a textile design studio, where he worked for sixteen years. During that time, he was conscripted into the British Army from 1948 to 1950, serving as a trooper in the Fifth Royal Inniskilling Dragoon Guards with the army of occupation in Germany.

In 1957, with poet Robin Skelton and painter Michael Snow, Connor founded the Peterloo Group of Manchester. The group was formed to bring together regional writers and artists, providing a community venue to share, discuss, and exhibit their works. The Peterloo Group became an important influence in the eventual formation of the Manchester Institute of Contemporary Arts.

After abandoning textile design, Connor taught life drawing at an art school and cake design at a bakery, leading to a position teaching liberal studies at Bolton Technical College. In his mid-twenties, he began to write poems, which led to his first publication in 1962. During the 1960s, Connor married and became a father to two sons and a daughter. In 1967, he earned a non-traditional M.A. at the University of Manchester and was invited to teach in the United States, where he worked for a year as Writer in Residence at Amherst College in Massachusetts.

Following Amherst, Connor returned to England for two years and turned his attention to theatre. He wrote several plays for children and adults which were performed professionally on the British stage. While commissioned to write a play for BBC Television, he also became an anchorman on a nightly magazine program for Granada Television.

In 1971, Connor returned to the United States as a Professor of English at Wesleyan University. There, he taught writing and ran a studio theatre devoted to producing student-written drama. In 1974, he was elected a Fellow of the Royal Society of Literature. The McPherson Library at the University of Victoria holds a selection of his papers and, his first love being art, a number of Connor's paintings reside in private and public collections. He became an American citizen in 1982 and retired from Wesleyan in 1998. He currently lives in Middletown, Connecticut.

www.ingramcontent.com/pod-product-compliance
Lightning Source LLC
Chambersburg PA
CBHW030459010526
44118CB00011B/1009